AN INTRODUCTION TO
THE COMMUNIST PARTY OF IRELAND

DUBLIN:
COMMUNIST PARTY OF IRELAND
2014

Communist Party of Ireland
James Connolly House
43 East Essex Street
Dublin 2

PO Box 85
Belfast BT1 1SR

www.communistpartyofireland.ie

ISBN 978-0-904618-60-0

Cover design by Paul Kirby

Introducing the Communist Party of Ireland

This booklet is intended to give a brief introduction for those interested in knowing more about the Communist Party of Ireland. We wish to introduce people to the ideas, policies and values of the CPI, to help those who are beginning to explore alternative politics for the first time to gain a fuller understanding of what we stand for, and to give those who are considering joining our party a brief overview of our policies and our strategy.

There are many false perceptions about what communists stand for, and these are constantly promoted by the establishment and its media. These falsehoods are part and parcel of a deliberate strategy by the elite to sow confusion and to blow smoke in people's eyes, to sustain and strengthen the belief among working people and in particular among the youth that there is no alternative to capitalism.

We hope this introduction will help clarify some basic principles and leave you with a better understanding of what we stand for and will encourage you to explore further the policies and strategy of the CPI, which are given more fully in the political documents adopted at the national congresses of our party.

What is the Communist Party of Ireland?

The Communist Party of Ireland is an all-Ireland party made up of working people whose policy is based on the theory of Marxism and whose objective is to be in the forefront in abolishing capitalism and building socialism. It actively works for the unity of all our people, regardless of national origins, religious affiliation, sex, or colour.

The CPI is a party of and for working people it is on the side of workers on the many issues and problems that face our people.

The CPI is rooted in Ireland's revolutionary history and its struggle for independence, and it has been an integral part of the labour movement and people's struggles since its foundation. The first Irish communist party, founded in 1921, took part in the War in Defence of the Republic, 1922–23; the foundation members included Roddy Connolly (son of James Connolly), Seán McLaughlin (surviving commandant of the 1916 Rising), and the writer Liam O'Flaherty.

The party played a leading role in the united actions of Protestant and Catholic workers in the North in the 1930s, was the organiser of the contingent of Irish volunteers who went to Spain to fight against fascism, was the force behind the unemployed movement in the 1950s, made a significant contribution to the reunification of the Irish trade union movement in 1959, was the driving force behind the establishment of the Northern Ireland Civil Rights Association and a leading component of Dublin Housing Action Committee in the 1960s, campaigned for world peace during the worst period of the "Cold War," led the Irish Voice on Vietnam in the 1960s and 70s, opposed Ireland's membership of what would become the European Union, and played an active role in the Irish Anti-Apartheid Movement.

The CPI was the first organisation to call for repudiating the unjust debt that has been placed on the backs of the people in order to pay off the corporate debt to foreign banks.

What is socialism?

A socialist society is one in which publicly owned and controlled enterprises become the dominant form of ownership in the economy under a government made up of the organised working people. This need not exclude some forms of private ownership continuing to exist for a considerable time.

Economic planning is necessary in a socialist society to prevent the booms and slumps that are a persistent feature of capitalism. Centralised planning enables the best use to be made of the country's resources and the technical skill of its workers and to protect the needs of the people as a whole. Socialism makes all economic, political, social and cultural areas of life subject to full democratic accountability, with the active participation of the people. Nothing and no-one should be beyond accountability to the people.

A socialist government will insist on the peaceful, negotiated settlement of international disputes and will consistently support international disarmament. Aggression and interference in the internal affairs of other countries will be replaced by a policy of friendship, non-interference, and mutual respect.

What is the difference between communists and socialists?

Communists believe that socialism can be achieved only if the working class wins state power and uses that power to abolish capitalism. The CPI openly declares what it stands for, and it struggles to win working people to that understanding. Among those who call themselves socialists there is a great divergence of opinion on what they stand for, ranging from the far-left parties and groupings to social democrats.

Historically there was no difference between communists and socialists. However, from the end of the nineteenth century, and even more so from the beginning of the First World War, the working-class movement has been divided into two main currents, with one section, which retained its revolutionary position, declaring themselves communists and the other current generally calling themselves socialists or social democrats. Within that current there is no agreement either on what socialism is or on how it can be achieved. In the main, however, those elements argue for collaboration with the capitalist class in order to achieve reforms that somehow will lead to socialism without a revolutionary struggle, which often leads them to argue for some form of better, fairer capitalism. Most social-democratic parties, including the Irish Labour Party, have long since abandoned any ideological commitment to socialism, while among other socialists there is a degree of confusion about what they stand for or how change can be brought about or even the nature of that change.

Communism is a very advanced form of human society that Marxists believe will evolve gradually from fully developed socialism, after all traces of capitalism and capitalist relations have been eliminated. In a communist society there will be no antagonistic classes and therefore no state apparatus (such as armies, police, and prisons), and all wealth-producing property will be owned in common. Under socialism the guiding principle is "to each according to their work"; under communism it will be "to each according to their needs." Exactly what such a future society will be like we can only guess at. There is no blueprint for it, nor are we concerned about speculating on this: our task is to defeat capitalism and pave the way for socialism.

Communists do not struggle to bring about communism: they struggle to bring about socialism, which will eventually develop into communism.

What is Marxism? Why should a political party be guided by it?

Beginning in the 1840s, Karl Marx and Frederick Engels developed a philosophy, a theory of history, a critique of political economy and a political programme based on a rational and scientific study of society and history. They showed that the history of all human societies has been a history of class struggle, that the way in which wealth is produced and controlled decides the nature and characteristics of a society, and in particular that the working class—the only class in history that does not exploit any other class—must set about the task of abolishing capitalism in order to end exploitation and oppression. For this reason the working class needs its own revolutionary political party.

Marxist theory has been enriched and extended by the theoretical work and the practice of other revolutionaries, notably V. I. Lenin and including our own James Connolly. In particular, Connolly led the way in developing a Marxist policy for a colonial and neo-colonial country, demonstrating the importance of understanding that the struggle for national independence and the struggle for socialism are two aspects of a single process.

Does the CPI advocate revolution?

Revolution is the transfer of political power from a ruling class to a more progressive class. Socialist revolution is the winning of state power by the working class.

Revolution is not the same as a revolt or an insurrection, nor does it necessarily involve the use of physical force—though history shows us that any significant advance by the working class or other progressive forces is likely to be met by violent opposition and repression, which the revolutionary movement must defeat. The CPI, therefore, is a revolutionary party.

Can there not be a mix of socialism and capitalism?

The essential fact relating to socialism is that the state is run and controlled by working people; and this requires a fundamental change in the nature of the state. A socialist state owns and controls the major industrial enterprises, public utilities (electricity, gas, water, transport, and communications), natural resources, the health service, and all other basic services that the people depend on, and runs them in the interests of the working people.

In the early period of socialist transformation there may be a case for some forms of productive private property; the extent of this would be the outcome of deep and meaningful debate among the people. The CPI does not think that the state should necessarily own every corner shop. The history of the building of socialism shows that at certain crucial periods it required some degree of capitalist economic development in order to develop aspects of the economy, or joint enterprises with foreign companies to gain access to technologies and expertise; but always the workers' state must retain control.

It will be the state's role to implement the shared solidarity as decided by the people after the maximum democratic participation of working people through the fullest discussion and debate to ensure that investment priorities are as the people have decided. As Lenin put it, "Every cook must learn to run the state."

Hasn't communism been attempted before and failed?

Communism has not been attempted anywhere, nor could it be, as communism is an economic and social system of the distant future that will evolve out of socialism.

The process of building socialism was begun in several countries during the twentieth century, notably those in central and eastern Europe where German fascism was defeated by the Red Army. Under extremely difficult conditions, huge obstacles were overcome and huge achievements were made. Despite this, a combination of poorly understood problems, political mistakes and external aggression led to counter-revolutions in most of those countries, whereby the socialist system was overthrown and capitalism was aggressively reintroduced.

Much of the anti-communist propaganda pumped out by the establishment and its media is based on the false idea that an attempt was being made to construct a communist society, that is, one without a state apparatus and without differences in income. No society at the present time can be judged against such false criteria. This propaganda is accompanied by horror stories about injustice and oppression that for the most part are complete falsification.

The project of building socialism under the leadership of the working class has not been invalidated and in fact has been strengthened by recent history and current events. Those who organised celebrations over the abolition of the Soviet Union and other socialist states are now presiding over the greatest assault ever on the rights and conditions of working people. Anti-communist falsification is an essential part of this strategy, as it is necessary to convince people that no alternative form of society is possible.

What is the CPI's attitude to the Soviet Union?

The CPI consistently saw the Soviet Union and the other socialist countries as the builders of a new society that promised to free humanity from exploitation and oppression. It never expected this task to be easy or without setbacks, and it continues to recognise their historic achievements as far more significant than their faults and weaknesses.

The building of socialism in the Soviet Union took place in very difficult and dangerous conditions; its development was shaped by both internal and external factors. The Soviet Union emerged from the devastation—material and human—of the First World War in one of the most backward and underdeveloped countries in Europe. Its birth was immediately met with invasion by sixteen foreign powers—in the immortal words of Winston Churchill, "to strangle the Bolshevik baby in its cradle."

Having emerged from this ordeal, the Soviet Union had to set about building socialism under siege, in a hostile world. The "democratic" states' hatred of communism was so great that they were prepared to use even fascism to combat it. They even tolerated the Nazi assault on the Spanish Republic. In the end they were forced to ally themselves with the Soviet Union in order to defeat Nazism; and the same Winston

Churchill had to admit that it was the Soviet Union that "tore the guts out of the German Army." All this was while it strove to build a new society, to educate millions deprived of education, to give shelter to millions who had no homes, to raise the cultural level and make culture available to the people and to reflect the real living experience of the people. It created millions of jobs, built new cities and towns, schools, hospitals, and factories. It struggled to bring about equality between men and women and between the many nationalities within its borders.

At the same time the Soviet Union, later joined by the other socialist countries of eastern Europe, was giving material as well as moral support to workers around the world and to the people fighting for their freedom from colonial exploitation. It provided assistance to the forces of national liberation in Asia and Africa and supported and protected other countries that embarked on the road to socialism, including Cuba.

The economic and social advances made by working people under socialism created more favourable conditions and strengthened the hand of workers struggling to improve their living and working conditions under capitalism.

The class forces that socialism challenges, while physically trying to isolate and destroy the Soviet Union and other socialist countries, also created an anti-communist ideological industry. Its purpose is to win the battle of ideas, and its method is to poison public opinion by lies and innuendo. This industry is financed in the main by the United States and staffed and serviced by the academic establishment and "think tanks," often finding common cause with the anti-communist "left."

They wish to narrow discussion of the history of socialism to the intense economic and political struggles that took place in the Soviet Union in the 1920s and 30s, without reference to the international context. They reduce these events to the role and machinations of individuals. Their purpose is to obliterate the experience and the liberating role that socialism played in the twentieth century and continues to play in those countries that are building a new society for their people.

The history and experience of socialism in the twentieth century is contested. We are well aware that, in the construction of socialism, serious mistakes and also abuses took place, and we have no desire to understate the gravity of those events. Methods of work persisted that had a negative effect on democratic practice, a top-down approach that in the long run led to alienation and cynicism among workers, weaknesses that the enemies of socialism were able to use to undermine the system.

We strive to face this historical experience honestly. We try to understand the rich lessons to be learnt from the first attempts to build socialism. The anti-communist strategy, on the other hand, is designed to blacken socialism and to frighten people away from exploring alternatives to capitalism—a moribund and decaying system.

The West's policy of "anything but communism" has led it to support any and every anti-communist regime, including the most brutal tyrannies and fascist dictatorships as well as mediaeval Islamist terrorists such as Al Qa'ida. Even with the demise of the socialist countries the anti-communist industry continues to subvert the vision of a rational and just society. While this industry, aided by some on the far left, never changes its menu of "Stalinism," "Gulag socialism," "state capitalism," etc., socialist Cuba, with mass democratic participation, constantly renews and invigorates the practice of living socialism and inspires millions of people.

The enemies of socialism seek to bury the enormous achievements of the Soviet Union and other socialist countries. They wish to confine communists and the left to a historical trap; by controlling and shaping how workers understand the past they strive to shape and control the future.

There are rich lessons to be drawn from the experience of building socialism, from both its many successes and its failures, experience that the CPI tries to bring to bear in its day-to-day struggles.

What is the CPI's attitude to the present economic crisis?

The economic crisis was caused by inherent features of capitalism at its present stage: it was not caused by a handful of unscrupulous bankers, or by greed, as we are often told.

Crises are constant and recurring features of capitalism—part of the system, as natural to capitalism as breathing is to a person. The present crisis is one of a continuous cycle of booms and busts, from the 1790s, 1840s, 1880s, 1930s, 1970s and 1980s to the continuing and deepening crisis of 2008. Such crises produced great misery for working people, often leading to wars.

In recent years the state has actively intervened to stave off crisis by adopting laws and policies that defend the ruling class, implementing an all-out assault on the social and labour rights won by working people over the past century. Austerity is not a solution to the debt crisis: the debt provides an opportunity to impose austerity.

The CPI is completely opposed to paying the socialised corporate debt imposed on the Irish people, a debt that is not theirs. This corporate debt is being used as a means of undermining and rolling back workers' wages and conditions and justifying savage cuts in public services and social welfare.

What is the CPI's attitude to the European Union?

The European Union (originally the Common Market, later the European Economic Community) was primarily established as a bulwark against socialism and the Soviet Union and to prevent the emergence of a strong left and workers' movement in western Europe after the Second World War. From the beginning its purpose has been to concentrate power at the centre, in the form of the EU Commission. There has been a step-by-step tightening of control at the centre, removing more and more political, economic and social decision-making from member-states, most strategically away from democratic accountability or influence at the national level, away from national class struggles, and concentrating them in Brussels.

This has resulted in domination by the major economic powers at the heart of Europe as well as the creation of structures that facilitate corporate lobbyists, such as the the European Round Table of Industrialists. The whole process has been to subordinate the interests of working people to the interests of the big monopolies. The EU is using the present economic crisis to further consolidate its control over member-states, particularly the peripheral states, turning that relationship of dependence into a new form of neo-colonialism within the structures of the EU itself.

The CPI opposed Ireland's membership of the Common Market, as it understood what the consequences would be for the social and economic interests of the people. It also opposed it because of the threat it posed to Irish democracy, sovereignty, and neutrality. Experience has borne out the CPI's grave concerns about the effect membership would have on the economic, social, cultural and political life of our country.

The EU is now in the process of building its own military forces to project and protect its global interests, which will most certainly mean the formal end of Irish military neutrality.

The Irish political establishment have been willing and active partners in the whittling away of national democracy and sovereignty. It is more important to the elite to actively maintain their economic and political relationship with the EU than to protect the interests of the Irish people. This is most clearly exposed in the imposition of the socialised corporate debt on the people.

For these reasons the CPI continues to oppose membership of the EU, as experience shows that to advance to socialism we need to break the stifling anti-people grip that Brussels has on the people. To solve the grave economic and social crisis in our country we need a different direction and different policies, which at present are restricted or outlawed under the EU treaties. The CPI believes that the Irish people must have the final say on all decisions that affect their economic and social interests, free from external dictates and bullying.

The CPI struggles to defend political independence and national sovereignty against the marginalising and dependence being imposed by the EU. It stands for equality between countries and peoples, for working-class patriotic internationalism.

What is imperialism?

During the nineteenth century, colonialism—the conquest and direct control of other countries and the seizing of their resources—developed into imperialism. Direct control by military and political means was not always necessary and where possible was replaced with economic control, whereby the huge American and European corporations gain ownership of the wealth of other countries under the guise of "investment"—backed up, where necessary, by military force.

Capitalism developed from a competitive local system into an all-embracing global system, divided among dominant countries and among monopoly companies. Through competition, companies either grew, by means of acquisition or mergers, or closed down, leading to a few corporations dominating markets. Monopoly—the opposite of competition—is in fact a result of competition.

To continue expanding, companies merged so as to better exploit foreign regions; and to support this process they required bank capital. Lenin described this process as the development of finance capital. Its expansion required the active support of states in suppressing revolts as well as in conquering new territories. Imperialism divided the world among the dominant powers; and any attempted redivision would result in war, as happened, for example, with the outbreak of the First World War in 1914.

The additional profits yielded from the super-exploitation of colonies provided the means to buy off workers in the metropolitan countries, which resulted in the split in the international socialist movement and the rise of the reformist tendency known as social democracy.

In the twentieth century, the process of merger and monopolisation continued at an extraordinary rate, so that today, of an estimated 43,060 transnational corporations, 80 per cent are controlled by 730 entities, and 40 per cent of these are controlled by a mere 147 entities. Three-quarters of these controlling entities are banks and financial institutions.

In Ireland the economic crisis is made worse by the country's marginal position within an imperialist bloc, the European Union, as well as by the servility of its political class. This means that resistance to the crisis must be anti-imperialist, involving the defence of what remains of the country's national independence and sovereignty and opposition to the control over Ireland (and other countries) by the EU Commission, working hand in glove with corporate lobbyists—in short, the reconquest of Ireland.

At the present time social democracy is publicly critical of "austerity" but in practice supports the massive attacks on workers' living standards, cuts in social welfare, and the privatisation of public companies and services. Social democrats believe in some form of better, fairer capitalism—not its overthrow or abolition. Here in Ireland social democracy finds its political expression in such parties as the Labour Party. Through their influence within trade unions and other people's organisations, social democrats continue to narrow and contain the demands and aspirations of workers to within the system itself. At the international level they have propagated the dangerous illusion of humanitarian imperialism, leading them to be active supporters of wars of aggression and occupation.

What is the CPI's view on the reunification of Ireland?

Ireland was partitioned in 1922 in the interests of British imperialism. But the subjection of Ireland to imperialism involves much more than partition. Our people are subject to domination by the European Union, by the United States—through excessive dependence on American transnational corporations—and by continued British interference, particularly in the north of Ireland.

The two states established in Ireland to meet the interests and needs of British imperialism, and the two wings of the Irish capitalist class, nationalist and unionist, have served their class interests well, but both have absolutely failed the needs of working people. Partition has failed and has left a legacy of bitter division and a culture of dependence and economic subservience, resulting in continued mass unemployment, poverty, and mass emigration from the whole country. Working people, not the business classes, have paid the price for partition.

The CPI welcomed the Belfast Agreement as a positive step towards ending political violence and creating conditions for the potential development of political struggle and the mobilisation of the people. The party recognises the limitations of the agreement and continues to argue both against any continuation of the failed elitist military strategy and for a strategy to transcend the limitations and to struggle for a new democracy that ends British interference and establishes a new national democracy, centred on the people.

To struggle merely for unity of territory is something Irish communists have opposed and argued against. The CPI believes we need to put the economic and social interests of the people at the centre of any struggle to end imperialist domination and control, that Ireland without its people is meaningless.

The party campaigns against all forms of discrimination and sectarianism, no matter what its source or how it manifests itself. This puts the struggle to end partition firmly at the centre of the liberation of the people, particularly the liberation of the working class.

Resisting and ultimately defeating imperialism, which is an essential condition for the building of socialism, requires a strategy that confronts all imperialist controls, including those of the European Union, the United States, and Britain, even if the latter is a much-diminished influence. This requires mobilising the working class and all working people, small farmers, pensioners, unemployed people, and students.

Communists place the liberation of the Irish working class at the centre of the struggle to defeat imperialism. The reunification of Ireland will come about as a consequence of uniting the majority of the people, north and south, in a common anti-imperialist struggle.

What is the CPI's view on trade unions?

The CPI recognises the importance of workers being members of and active within trade unions. Trade unions are the most basic organisation of workers, for defending themselves from the arbitrary actions of employers. Experience has shown that workers can be mobilised to defend their interests and are willing to stand up when they are given a sense of direction, with clear demands, objectives, and leadership.

The CPI actively works for and encourages workers to join a trade union and to be active within it. The many weaknesses that in turn generate frustration among workers are no reason for not becoming involved. Workers can realise their own interests and full potential only when they combine with other workers in united action.

"Social partnership" has sapped the strength of the movement, has weakened trade union structures politically and industrially, has reduced direct participation by workers in their unions, and has resulted in the trade union movement becoming in some cases indistinguishable from the interests of employers and the state. "Social partnership," Croke Park Agreements and Haddington Road Agreements are the strategy of a weak and politically servile social-democratic trade union leadership.

The CPI stands for the fullest independence of the trade unions from the control and anti-union laws of the state. The communist approach to trade unions is to build the political and class understanding of workers, to show that they have different and separate interests from those of their employers and the state, to maximise democratic participation at all levels, and to build and strengthen links and co-operation between trade unions and the many community organisations and the struggles to defend and to fight for a shared future.

What is the CPI's view on women's equality?

The demand for full equality between men and women has been an essential part of communist and socialist thinking from the beginning. Indeed the movement for women's rights has its roots in the labour movement, in the struggles of women workers. It was the communist Clara Zetkin who first proposed the celebration of International Women's Day. Communist women played a leading role in establishing the celebration of International Women's Day in Ireland.

The CPI has consistently participated in the movement for women's rights—for equality in the work-place, in society and in the home and for a woman's right to the control of her own body, including the right to choose an abortion. This movement has achieved some advances, such as equal pay in many trades and professions; yet women remain severely disadvantaged at work, especially in low-paid work, where equal pay has not penetrated.

An important part of the struggle is opposition to the culture of machismo and misogyny, which is not only a legacy of the past but is increasingly propagated by the commercial mass media, reflecting the crisis of capitalism.

To these issues the CPI brings a socialist and working-class viewpoint, in contrast to those bourgeois feminists who talk of "glass ceilings" and who would be satisfied with equality in the boardroom, the professional classes, and the Dáil, leaving low-paid women workers as they are.

Capitalism can never provide true equality between men and women, because by its very nature it is based on the exploitation of the majority by a small minority. It does not care whether exploiters are men or women, so long as profit is accumulated. The full emancipation of women, as of men, cannot be achieved without advancing towards socialism.

Are communists opposed to religion?

No. The CPI regards religion as a private matter for each individual. It takes no interest in people's religious affiliation, including that of its own members. The party does not believe that the churches should be involved in running the state.

Communists work with progressive Christians and others who have made important contributions to the struggle of peoples against colonialism and imperialism. It is conscious of the commitment by people of religious faith to the struggle for peace and social justice.

It is true that clerical authorities, of all religions, have allied themselves with the oppressors and exploiters of peoples, advocating submission and obedience by the common people to their rulers. There has always been a conflict between them and the interests of the believers. Church leaders of all faiths have a tradition of opposing progressive change in society; there is an equally long tradition of revolt and rebellion against oppression expressed in religious terms. In present-day conditions these believers are potential allies, and potential members of our party.

What is the CPI's view on the environmental crisis?

The continuing destruction of the global environment is an inextricable part of modern monopoly capitalism. It is capitalism that is creating the environmental crisis, with its need for constant growth and its use of limited natural resources. If capital is to grow it must alienate and exploit both workers (in the form of their labour power) and the environment (in the form of the resources required and the pollution created by its methods of production).

The World Wildlife Fund has reported that air temperature in the Arctic has increased by an average of 5°C over the last hundred years, melting the polar ice caps at an incredible rate, to a point where there will be almost no summer sea ice left in the Arctic by 2020. This has severe implications for the world, not only in the loss of polar bear and seal habitats, and the consequent effects on local people, but in dramatic changes to the entire northern hemisphere. The lack of a permanent ice shield will result in the loss of other sea species and a general acceleration of global warming.

Climate change is only one critical issue facing humanity. Equally important, and linked with climate change, is the manner in which production is changing the land. Changes in land cover have resulted in three-quarters of ice-free land showing signs of human alteration, causing many environmental problems. It is the principal cause of the extinction of species, with 13 per cent of birds, 25 per cent of mammals and 41 per cent of amphibians now threatened with extinction.

Maintaining biodiversity is crucial for humankind, as natural ecosystems provide many life-sustaining resources, such as the pollination of food crops, the formation of soil, nutrient cycling, water supply, the treatment of residues, medical resources, and even food itself. The destruction of rainforests, especially in Brazil, is of particular concern, as deforestation is releasing huge amounts of carbon dioxide into the atmosphere, again speeding up climate change.

The list of environmental concerns is growing and now includes not only climate change but acidification of the seas, the destruction of species, shortages of freshwater, chemical pollution of the air, water, and soil, and now "extreme weather."

An additional significant factor in the pollution and destruction of the environment is modern imperialist warfare, including its use of depleted uranium in weapons. Military production is the most anti-environmental of all industries; and wars, of course, are hundreds of times worse.

While changing personal habits is a step along the road, it is not enough; and this approach shifts the burden and responsibility onto individuals, families, and communities, allowing the role and nature of capitalism itself off the hook. It is this system, the life-styles it promotes and the savage exploitation of our limited natural resources in the endless drive for super-profits that are the central problem.

We can understand the nature of the environmental catastrophe we face only if we link the nature and ownership of capitalist production with capitalist commodity fetishism and the life-styles and choices imposed on us. The crisis in the global environment will be reversed only if we fundamentally challenge capitalism itself.

The very future and survival of our planet and the lives of hundreds of millions of our fellow-citizens are bound up in the struggle for socialism. We cannot save our planet and save capitalism.

What is the difference between the CPI and other left parties? Could all the left parties not get together and agree on a common programme?

Political parties are organisations of people that share an analysis of their society and agree on a common strategy. No other party in Ireland has the same analysis of Irish society or the same approach to confronting imperialism.

The CPI is always ready to co-operate with other parties and organisations, but there is not enough common understanding to make a joint political programme possible at this time. On a variety of issues and campaigns it co-operates with other parties, organisations and individuals on the basis of mutual respect and agreed goals.

What are the CPI's activities?

The CPI is a party of working people for working people. It is a party of activists, who work in trade unions, community organisations, solidarity campaigns, cultural projects and other democratic movements as well as campaigns conducted by the party itself. It organises public meetings, maintains a bookshop in Dublin, and publishes pamphlets and periodicals, and it was the guiding force behind the setting up of a number of significant campaigning organisations.

How is the CPI organised?

Where there are enough members in a district the CPI organises them in branches; where there are individual members the party maintains as much contact as possible, so that every member can contribute, regardless of whether they live in a village or in a city. Collective action empowers the individual, draws on and maximises the experiences of the members, so that everyone can play their part and everyone can make a worthwhile contribution.

Branches elect their own chairperson and secretary and any other officers they require. Meetings include discussions of current developments and of the party's strategy and activities, in which all members can participate and express their views. Members are expected to be activists and to carry out decisions once they have been collectively discussed and decided by the party.

Members pay a small membership subscription, in proportion to their income.

A party congress, made up of representatives of all the members, is held every three or four years. The congress elects the National Executive Committee, which is the national leadership of the party.

Is the CPI a registered political party?

Yes. Registration does not confer any rights other than the privilege of having a party's name on the ballot paper in an election, while at the same time it imposes certain obligations, such as having to submit information about its financial affairs.

Does the CPI contest elections?

Yes. However, it does not limit its tactics to contesting elections, nor does it believe that this is the way in which the working class will win power in a capitalist country. On the other hand it can be a useful opportunity to get its message across to more people, to gain support, to mobilise its members and supporters, and to expose the weakness of the view that electoral success by itself can bring about radical change.

Elections and parliaments have an important place in the whole process of advancing the interests of the people, but only if this is linked to struggle by the people outside the parliamentary system. Marxists believe that the working class may achieve political power through a combination of means, including electoral means, when it has achieved mass support and when the ruling class is no longer able to maintain its control. Precisely how and when this will happen will depend on the conditions in a particular country at the time.

Is the CPI part of an international communist organisation?

No. There is no international organisation of communist parties (though there was at one time). On the other hand, all communist parties are